*This book is for all the magicians in Edinburgh,
especially Lel and Robin Blair, Marion Campbell,
Lynda Clark, Richard Mowe and my magical wife,
Regi Claire*

Contents

Acknowledgements   IX
Foreword   Donald Wilson   XI

🦢 MAGIC EDINBURGH

A Recipe for Whisky   I
The Magicians of Edinburgh   2
Dancing in Princes Street   5
Incident in Greyfriars Kirkyard   9
Oor Tram's Plea tae the Cooncillors o Edinburgh   II
Afternoon in a Café on the Royal Mile   14
Reclaiming St Andrews Square   16
A History of the Scottish Parliament   18
Kickstarting History   20
EH1 2AB   22
West Newington Place   24
Nicolson Square   25
Absolution on the Edinburgh City Bypass   26
Beware!   28
Not for Profit   30
Four Haikus for a New Year   32
Come Evening   33
How Can the Words I Love You . . .   34
McSonnet   35
Edinburgh is a Thousand Islands   36
Our Piece of Good Fortune   42
Something to Look Forward to   44
Incantation for a Good Voyage   45
Our City Listens to Itself   47

Going Breughel in Edinburgh   48
Homecoming   50
The Circle Dante Wasn't Shown   52
The Singing Butler   54

🦢 MUSIC EDINBURGH   63

Contemporary Music in Scotland   65
Haydn and Chemotherapy   66
The Time for Miracles   68
Three Composers Respond to the Politics of
    Perpetual War   71
Two of Cassandra's Songs   78
The Voice Inside   79

🦢 VIRTUAL EDINBURGH   85

The Other Edinburgh   86
David Hume Takes a Last Walk on Arthur's Seat   88
David Hume's History of Scottish Weather   91
The Completed Parthenon on Calton Hill   94
The Juggler of Greyfriars Kirkyard   96
The New Town's Response to the Threat of Global
Warming   98
Somewhere in these Sky-Blue Streets   102
The Gondolas of South Bridge   104
A Day in the Afterlife of Sir Walter Scott   106
A Proposal for Our City's Digital Upgrade   109
Edinburgh Love Song   112

Acknowledgements

Grateful thanks are due to the editors of the following publications where some of the poems first appeared: *Ambit, Edinburgh Review, Perspectives, The Big Issue in Scotland, New Writing Scotland, Northwords, Poetry Scotland, The Scotsman, Edinburgh Evening News, Where Rockets Burn Through – Contemporary Science Fiction Poetry from the UK*. Some poems were contained in *Without a Backward Glance* (Barzan Publishing). Some were set to music and included in CDs by Lyell Cresswell (*The Voice Inside*, Naxos) and Edward Harper (*Miracles*, Delphian). 'The Gondolas of South Bridge' was arranged by double-bassist Conrad Molleson for *Archipelago* on Radio Scotland. Several of the poems have been jazzed up by Dick Lee for *The Magicians of Edinburgh* on the Edinburgh Fringe Festival 2012. The title poem was made into a flash film by WordPowered for the British Council.

The author appreciates the commissioning of some poems by the Edinburgh Sick Kids Foundation, the Scotch Malt Whisky Society, the Saltire Society, Edinburgh Inspiring Capital for the Round the World Yacht Race, the City of Edinburgh Council, the Edinburgh UNESCO City of Literature Trust, the Edinburgh Hogmanay Party, *Scotland on Sunday*, Scottish PEN, the Scottish Government (Culture Division), the Scottish Poetry Library and BBC Radio 3 and 4.

The author would also like to thank the Scottish Arts Council (now Creative Scotland) for a Writer's Bursary, the Cove Park International Artist Residency Centre and the Ledig-Rowolt Foundation (the Château de Lavigny in Switzerland), all of whose generosity allowed him time to complete this book. He is also most grateful to the Royal Literary Fund for a Fellowship at Edinburgh University's Office of Lifelong Learning.

Foreword

It is my great pleasure to offer a few words of introduction to this celebration of Edinburgh. Ron Butlin is our Makar, our Poet Laureate, and these poems revel in many aspects of our city – its inhabitants both past and present, its history, its contemporary life and sometimes even its imagined future!

Whatever the theme, Butlin's playful flights of fancy, though always entertaining, usually have a serious purpose. The Parthenon on Calton Hill is still being completed, apparently – by ghosts! Having stepped down from his monument to visit the new Parliament, Sir Walter Scott has come to his own conclusions about the changes. There is a recipe for whisky, a virtual river running through Princes Street Gardens, Greyfriar's Bobby gets a mention and so, of course, do the trams . . .

Those of us who live here know Scotland's capital to be so much more than a city with 'wall-to-wall festivals' gift-wrapped in its past for the many tourists who enjoy a short stay here. From the furthest outskirts to the very centre, Edinburgh is vibrant with business, with education and research, law and government. It is multi-layered in every sense and, with surely one of the grandest skylines to be seen anywhere in the world, combines Georgian elegance with modern concepts. Like any city Edinburgh has its problems, however, which Butlin does not ignore. He describes it as a place 'of possibilities and prohibitions'.

With the debate about our nation's future now getting underway, this book is a welcome contribution to what really lies at the heart of that discussion – our identity, both national *and* local.

Donald Wilson, THE LORD PROVOST OF EDINBURGH

Magic Edinburgh

A Recipe for Whisky

Wring the Scottish rain clouds dry;
take sleet, the driving snow, the hail;
winter twilight; the summer's sun slowed down
to pearl-sheen dusk on hillsides, city-roofs,
on lochs at midnight.
And, most of all, take the years that have already run
to dust, the dust we spill behind us . . .

All this, distil. And cask. And wait.
The senselessness of human things resolves
to who we are – our present fate.
Let's taste, let's savour and enjoy.
Let's share once more.
Another glass for absent friends. Pour
until the bottle's done.

Here's life! Here's courage to go on!

Many years ago I lived in a flat off Morrison Street. When I returned to Edinburgh after an extended period abroad, I found that part of the city to have changed beyond recognition. The magicians, however, remain.

The Magicians of Edinburgh

Our Late Medieval cobbled-together city of kirkyards,
     cathedrals,
howffs, castles, closes, courts, vennels and wynds,
hay markets, grass markets, flesh markets
managed to hit the twenty-first century
– running!

How come?
How come our rudely interrupted parliament talks twice as
     much sense
(or talks twice as fast)? To make up for lost time?
How come trams and pavement tables are reclaiming our
     streets?
How come there is shopping 24/7, pubbing, clubbing and all-
     night kebabs?
Wall-to-wall festivals? Bus lanes and wheelie bins?
The Hogmanay Party?

Did a sorcerer step out of a book of old Scottish folk tales,
take a 35 in from the airport, flash his Day-Saver Ticket,
to end up in the Southside at no extra cost?
Did Seventies' Edinburgh shock him *so* much?

The boarded-up windows, the litter, graffiti,
the horses hauling themselves and their carts out on their
    rounds,
their breath clouding the cold morning air, and Sir Sean
    Himself
riding high on the milk crates?
Did one wave of a corporate wand turn soot-blackened
tenements and windowless pubs into these glass –
and-mirror palaces? (Banks, insurance, law and pensions
– for who else retains sorcerers these days?)

Magic happens daily on the Bridges, on George Street,
in Tollcross, a nod from a stranger,
a quick drink with a friend I've bumped into.
(I never leave home, but meet someone I know.)
From my Newington flat the Forth's a Mediterranean blue,
there are faraway hills I can sometimes almost touch . . .

Most of all, when I stand at the top of the Mound, perfectly
    positioned
between God's law and Man's (the Kirk to my left,
the Bank to my right) I see our city shaped by the sky
and the sky by our city, and heaven itself seems possible then,
if only for a moment, and if only I would let it.

Tenement City. Corporate City. Capital City. Festival City.
World Heritage City, UNESCO City of Literature.
We don't need street maps or SatNav to find where
    our friends live.

Together, we are the magicians and we make the city.

All Edinburgh is ours – and it's personal!

Edinburgh's city centre has been brought to a standstill on many occasions, usually celebratory, but not always. There was once an anarchists' rally I found myself drawn into, and, of course, there are always the trams . . .

Dancing in Princes Street

I. FIRST DANCE (Scottish Country Dancing)

A clown in face-paint, kilt and trainers. Bagpipes.
Standing legs apart to blow strathspeys and reels
the full length of Princes Street while clowns and fairies
heel-and-toe the stationary afternoon, strip the willow
between deserted traffic islands and summer-yellow
windowless police vans. Fluttering their paper wings.
Sunlight on their stardust skin.
Handclapped time comes shuddering back
from boarded-up shop windows, steel-barricaded shop
    doors.
Laughter's shredded by helicopter blades.

Meanwhile, the likes of you and me look on, penned in
behind the RSA pillars for our comfort and security.
So many wallflowers at the dance.

2. SECOND DANCE (Slow)

Leaving Stockbridge at three a.m., grabbing the after-hours
    funicular
that runs from Lyell and Catherine's up to George Street,
the Mound, The Meadows and home.

Halfway there, the Rioja running out on us, our effortlessly
    upwards glide
jams, shudders. Gears lock. Traction slips, and one of us
nearly hits the cobbles . . .

A few stumble-steps later we spread our wings.

Soaring high above Princes Street, gliding north,
south, east and west –

Following the unseen ley-lines of our city and the unspoken
certainties of our heart, we'll never fear a fall to earth.

3. THIRD DANCE (Hokey-cokey)

Time for the formal ball, invitation only.

Dress code: fluorescent orange and hard hats. Health &
    Safety boots.
Clipboards for the dance cards.

The first band strikes up –

The second band strikes up –

The third band strikes up –

One, two, three and –

You dig a big hole here, you dig a big hole there,
you dig the biggest hole ever and another as a spare.
You shut the city down, take a six-month break
& that's what it's all about!

Hey!

You plan a tram route up, you plan a tram route down,
You plan another plan for the centre of the town,
You rip the new line out and you start it all again
& that's what it's all about!

Hey!

4. THE LAST DANCE

The first black wall moves closer. Then the second.
The third.

The woman PC's so young she needs only pigtails and a
        brace
to look her real age. What music did *she* hear back in
        Primary –

saying *Yes* when asked to dance the black-walled dance,
saying *No* to stardust and wings?

She strolls over to the wallflowers –
Careful, sir, my colleagues will be moving in soon.

Meanwhile the black visors, body armour, shields,
    batons, boots.
What music will *they* dance to? What steps
have *they* learned?

Greyfriars Bobby was a Skye Terrier (1856–72) who remained
guarding the grave of his dead master for fourteen years, never
quitting his post except when he heard the One o'Clock Gun and
would then go off to eat. An extraordinary example of loyalty
and devotion.

Incident in Greyfriars Kirkyard

Finding myself near the kirkyard one afternoon, I
    went in
to look for my grandfather, pay my respects.
Couldn't find him. Soon the rain was battering down like
    you've never seen.
Any more of this, I'm thinking as I turn and head back to
    the gate,
and I'll be moving in here myself.

That's when I saw something lying on a gravestone
like someone had flung it there.

Raining cats and dogs, all right! Next thing,
I'm getting the hard stare.
Lost, are you? I'm bending down, reaching forward to –
when that sodden-wet bundle, head sheltered between its
    front paws,
goes nose-to-tail rigid as stone itself saying, No.
Saying, Leave me. Saying, Go away and leave me.

The whole afternoon stopped. The kirkyard,
    the hammering rain,
the cold dead chill coming up from the ground – all of it
stopped right there and then. That's how it was.

Me staring down at that mossed-over gravestone, at that
    small dog.
And him lying all on his own forever, it seemed,
but not alone.

For part of 2010, a section of tram stood on its rails at the foot of the Mound, an exhibit of the good times to come. After enduring rain, sleet, tourists and irate bus drivers for several months, it was removed. The tracks were then lifted . . . To date, no one has seen a tram since.

Oor Tram's Plea tae the Cooncillors o Edinburgh

I'm scunnered wi gaitherin stour an decay,
wi blocking up Princes Street, wastin away,
gang naewhere, daein nowt, nae staps an nae route,
whiles wunnering whit bein a tram's aa aboot.
Sae dinna dash past till ye hear ma travails
– it's no me, I'm thinkin, that's ganged aff the rails!

Forbye that I'm sleek in ma chic Sunday best,
that I'm wired up an sat-navved, ma hairt's sair
    distressed.
Fer I canna begin if I'm no right plugged in
an ma stairt button's no bin pressed!

It's no a tram that I am but a PR-type sham,
a 'no-motion' notion, a 'concept' on wheels.
Try it yersel and see hou it feels
tae be dumped in the street, left aa on yer ain.
Fenced in. Locked up, in sunshine or rain.
I'll soon stairt tae rust, tae creak an grow auld,
anither year's passed – an no yin ticket sold!

Shoppers aa shun me an bus drivers curse,
Tourists staun gawkin, they mock me . . . an worse:
'This cab's sitting empty. There's no cables above.'
Then pretendin tae pity oor tram-challenged city,
they offer tae gie me a shove!

In ma dreams I see rooms fou o lawyers aa gabbin,
there's cash fleein aaweys, an everyin's grabbin
at fifties in fistfous tae cover their fee,
while naethin moves forrad – least of aa, me!

Ma nightmare turns scary as yin claps his hands:
'It's high time we scrapped these extravagant plans.
Instead, keep that tram to the centre of town,
Princes Street up . . . and Princes Street down.
A few stops for the shops and somewhere to park it . . .
Waverley Steps, say, then back to Haymarket.'

Nae wunner I'm sufferin low self-esteem,
I'm the joke o the city frae Leith tae Balgreen.
The ridicule's public, there's naewhere tae hide
frae the Cooncil Tax payers I've taen fer a ride.

꩜

Cooncillors, please, I'm doun on ma knees
(on ma wheels I should say!), beggin ye: Seize
whae's in chairge by the scruff o their necks,
bang heids th'gither until somethin brecks,
mak guid common sense oot o mismanaged hash,

then sort oot this fankled up, legal stramash!
Inspire them, or fire them, or threaten the jail
if they dinna get back tae layin mair rail!

Oor city's been patient, but its patience is done:
it's fed up o the mess an the mair mess tae come.
An I'm fed up, tae. I maun stairt on ma route
afore the track's lifted an I'm cancelled oot!

Edinburgh has so many histories – and they're all around us. It was only recently I learned that John Knox had been a galley slave . . .

Afternoon in a Café on the Royal Mile

Listen hard enough, you'll hear the double-handed hack of
    claymores
on the Castle battlements, stacked wood and righteousness
catching fire, the *thump-thump-thump* of Nasmyth's steam-
    hammer,
the soundless rush of the Higgs particle and Dolly's
very first bleat. That's the past for you – so much background
    clamour
to our pavement-table beer.

Nearby, in St Giles, John Knox's pulpit strains
against its moorings. Listen hard enough, you'll hear the hiss
    of warm rains
hitting overheated earth, and ice-floes breaking
off, and chunks of Arctic slowly drifting south. Bent double,
Knox hauls back his weight in hatred –
galley oar blistering his palms, iron fetters
scraping his ankles raw. He rows because he has to –
the stubbornness of open sea, the unrepentant shore.
Who's standing at the wheel, who'll navigate such wrecked
and chartless waters – *His* God? Someone else's? None?

No problem. Not for us. These days the universe and
    more
is at our fingertips, we're only a mouse-click from
    salvation.

DELETE –

An afternoon with friends among our city's medieval
    wynds and closes.
From time to time, fifteen-storey tenements come
    crashing down harmlessly
upon our heads. History's worn lightly here, it's lived in.
The High Street runs straight from Robert Bruce
to Deacon Brodie, Scott, Simpson,
Elsie Inglis . . . and so on down to *us*.
We check his dates and theirs, on Google.
We check our own.

DELETE –

Strip away the buildings, the well-intentioned parks, the
    locked-up
doorways. By now we surely know what's bearable,
and what we can survive.

DELETE –

The threatened rain has come to nothing.
We need to stand up for a moment – our pavement table's
needing moved again to catch the early evening sun.

St Andrew Square had been long closed to the general public. A ceremony involving, among others, First Minister Alex Salmond and myself, marked its transformation into an official Poetry Garden. More recently it was home to tents of the OCCUPY movement.

Reclaiming St Andrew Square

For the last few centuries the mausoleum-heavy stonework of
    the New Town
has loaded shops and offices, millionaire flats and
basements onto these long-ago green slopes.

No mighty flowing river, but junctions and roundabouts, bus
    lanes
and parking meters. Statues of the great and good
look down on us, checking the streets don't cross each other
simply for the fun of it,
and that you and I don't lose ourselves
in one another's dreams.

Whatever. The combined weight of these department stores,
banks and corporate headquarters
keeps everything in its place.

Ours is a city of possibilities and prohibitions where
we do our best to find the best way forward
and seek out kindness where we can.

But only in these very public gardens,
only in the green spaces of these very public gardens,
can we feel the living earth beneath us. Its reassurance.

And so, let's pause a moment here, draw strength –
and reclaim what is ours.

After a near 300-year interruption, the Scottish Parliament once
again sat in Edinburgh. It was a new start for us all, and especially
for the many new MSPs who had given up non-political jobs to help
govern.

A History of the Scottish Parliament

God's first week was a busy one:
universal chaos, light and darkness, stars, planets
and attendant moons (the Divine Breath occasionally
lending atmosphere), oceans, continents and so on . . .
Come Sunday He stayed in bed.

Time (that shove of Divine Encouragement, turning
what might otherwise have stayed a hobby
into something with a future) began to pass.
The senseless destiny of things took up more and more Space.
Life, and then death – all in the blink of an innocent eye.

Counting backwards through the Tribes of Israel's begats
and begones, Bishop Ussher dated God's Last Laugh
at 4004 BC. The rest is history.
Fast forward through that blur of good and bad intentions
(the fewer people taking part the better

chance for love) to Scotland, 1999.
We vote, we count. Peter Pan and Wendy grow up
overnight. They're forced to. Sudden, though:
no adolescence, no trying out new looks, new styles,
new attitudes. No chance to practise who they are.

Instead, from Day One, a job, a diary to be filled.
Adult responsibilities. A place of their very own, a house
that's so brand new it's still a *concept*,
like 'the future' (that darkest continent at whose borders
we fret away our lives), like 'Scottish identity'.

God's work done and dusted, he left the building. We're
    on our own.
The history we make, will make us in return …

*More than ten years after the opening of the new Scottish Parliament
... and where are we?*

Kickstarting History

Several centuries ago Scotland found itself drawn
into another country's slipstream.
Our history shut down.

We breathed dead air. Whole villages collapsed into rubble,
fields wasted to empty moorland, mountains retreated
to wrap themselves in cloud, lochs swallowed down curses
and their waters turned black.
Families were split, clans broken up
and the human wreckage scattered
to the winds. What was left was still a country,
but only just.

In the last year of the last millennium we summoned up our
        strength –
we sidestepped the slipstream.
Kickstarted our history.

Like it or not, we're on the move again, all of us:
the families, the clans, the country.
No one can see into the future, no one can go ahead
and check things out on our behalf.

And as for all we've been through, the cost
paid by generation after generation
of people just like us?

If we're lucky, our past will bear us company.

When a homeless person dies with no means of identifying them, they are referred to by the relevant post code. A few years ago a beggar was discovered in Lothian Road – she had frozen to death.

EH1 2AB

If I had sat down in Lothian Road this afternoon,
cross-legged on the pavement,
the stone wall behind me –

If I had placed a plastic cup in front of me
and a blanket round
my shoulders –

If the hours had been the east wind cutting
the length of the street
while the cold hardened into me –

If the day could not have been different, or the date
or the clouds or the sleet
or the rain –

If I'd stopped looking round me at faces,
at people; if I'd stopped staring down
at my uncovered hands –

If I had been sitting up straight
when they asked me to move –

If I'd still been sitting up straight when they touched
my shoulders to wake me –

❧

A woman. A plastic cup. A blanket.
The pavement.
The wall.

They told her she had to move on.
She said nothing.
They asked her her name.
She said nothing.

❧

A hospital sheet to cover her face.
Her ankle tagged to record the location
of where she was found –

A postcode to stand for her name
when at last she's given
a place of her own.

West Newington Place

He's curled at the edges, broken-spined and ready
to be withdrawn from circulation;
few have glanced beyond the early chapters;
the end will come as a surprise to no one.
He's on loan, as it were, to a public who've stopped
reading books like him.
Date-stamped all those years ago, then carelessly
corrected, smudged and scribbled over –
the clear print's blurred to tiredness,
hesitation, an apology.

From what I saw today the pages are slipping out of sequence;
the story's making less and less sense.
Who can gather up the leaves, who can put them
in some sort of order?

There is no other copy to refer to.

Nicolson Square

The girl's left hand keeps her coat shut, the other's
empty. She's standing in the middle of the street,
the traffic breaking to a stop around her.
Hardly sixteen – bleached hair, bleached skin, fear.

The man she's with – badly healing cuts and anger
clenched into a face, pressed-in bruises
where the eyes should be.
She's telling him she's sorry, and being sworn at.

Nearby, a parliament of two men and a woman sits
    arguing
upon the pavement; they shout at her to grow up,
can't she? A taxi horn blares.
She doesn't move.

I drop my 50p into the parliamentary cup, and walk past.
Behind me, the street shuts like a book, the place marked
just at the point where he hits her
in the mouth.

When I'm back this evening, the story will have moved on.
No girl, no man and no parliament – only you and I
and everyone else, and the street growing darker around us
as the sun abandons it.

Absolution on the Edinburgh City Bypass

This is the *rush* hour? – this slow-moving procession of men
    and women seated
as if in sedan chairs carried by invisible bearers?

Well, our bearers seemed to have walked off and left us. We're
    stuck.
Gridlocked in that no man's land between the Lasswade
and Straiton turn-offs. Have our bearers headed for the hills?
Migrated? Taken our jobs, our wives, our homes?
Hijacked our evenings and weekends?
Replanned the slip roads so we go round
and round in circles?
Retilted the Earth so the tides will always run against us?
One thing's for sure – they've reset its rotation.
Each minute's been slowed down to an hour
and that hour to a year.
There'll be no tomorrow between Lasswade and Straiton,
not in our lifetime.

We'll watch the stars repattern themselves, cancelling out
    our birth.
Some Divine Hand or other will do the rest – a clean sweep,
and we're gone. An absolution of sorts.

Until that moment comes, however, we're stranded here, at a
    standstill –
struggling to remember who we are and where we're going.

    But we *will*
remember – like it or not, we always do.
Then, with a sudden shudder that catches us unawares,
we'll move forward half a metre,
half a metre nearer home.

Edinburgh is a historic city of ghosts and spirits, many of them still haunting the wynds and closes of the Old Town. Coming home late on a dark, dark night, you can still sense them. This was surely the real inspiration for Stevenson's Dr Jekyll and Mr Hyde.

Beware!

Whoever crosses us – beware!
Whoever tip-toes past, take care
we don't come tip-toe after
in the dark. Your street, your stair,

your floor. Our soundless tread
soon takes us to your door.
Locks? Keys? Our mind need only seize
upon this clumsy world, then ease
it, bend it to our will.

We reach inside and slide the dead
bolt back – effortless and slow.
It is enough we *want* it so.
                              Stay still,
sleep on. Things are always as they seem
to the dreamer safe within the dream.

Your curtained room, your bed.
No words of comfort, grace
or blessing comes from us – instead,
we are shadow cast across your face,
a darkness seeping in . . .

(Elsewhere, your bedside clock ticks
laboured time, stuttering
on until all's done.)

. . . to let our one and only life begin.

Politicians and artists do not always see eye to eye, so I was delighted when the Great and the Good down at Holyrood commissioned a version of this poem to preface a government paper on arts funding. Only time will tell if they got my message . . .

Not for Profit

Once upon a time the king took on an orchestra,
the prince a school of painters, lesser gentry settled for
a poet or two. While History went on horseback
the Arts kept pace, more or less.
Wars were fought, gods demanded sacrifice –
Let loose the bards! they cried, and the enemy was surely
    done for,
in a tangle of harp strings and curses.

Ah, those were the days – when serious things
were taken seriously!

The year is 2010. No king,
no warrior prince to speak of, the *nouveau* gentry need
accountants, roomfuls of
accountants. And lawyers. And more
lawyers. Wars are lobbied for, gods go armed,
and children get blown to Kingdom Come
on a daily basis.

Seen from the comfort of History's stretch limo
– that soundless glide of tinted glass, of black and bullet-
    proof
conviction – the Arts might soon become a passing blur,
just as the poor have always been.

Most bankers' individual bonuses are several times the
    budget
for our nation's literature. The greediest threaten
to leave the country? Let's pack their bags for them!

That long-ago king knew well a nation's arts
are a nation's best PR. And cost-effective.
Artists are not for sale, of course, but they come cheap –
ridiculously cheap when set against the going rate
for consultants, say. Or cluster bombs. Or nuclear upgrades.

Please don't think of us as businessmen. We're not.
Yet we're always on the make – with heart and soul
we're making Scotland's music, Scotland's poetry,
paintings, plays . . .

Not for profit, but for us all.

Haikus from eleven Scottish writers were commissioned for the Edinburgh New Year's Day celebrations (1/1/11). The short poems were looped for continuous display on a gloriously mega-sized plasma screen erected next to the RSA Gallery in Princes Street.

Four Haikus for a New Year

1.

The Old Year warns – *Don't go!* The New Year welcomes so, so seductively . . .

2.

Pause. Breathe. In. Out. Pre- pare the sounding board you'll be for the pell-mell bells.

3.

Lay down the Old Year like stone, like dead weight. Raise up the New Breath of Life.

4.

Last year's rain will soon cease falling forever. Next year's sunlight – your eyes!

This poem came to me, almost complete, as I was returning from town one day across the Meadows. Not having pen and paper with me, I really speeded up to reach home before I forgot it. The subject came out of nowhere and has nothing to do with the park I was in, nor the time of day. But there it was – somewhere between Middle Meadow Walk and Newington.

Come Evening

The morning before, the morning to come.
The restless sky, the hesitant sun.
Light returning us each to our birth.
Stars sown in black, black earth.

Our lives are ourselves foreshortened, while we
look on – and curse and bless, and make promises.

Hoping that you and I . . .

Hoping that he and she . . .

Come evening comes forgiveness.

The winner of a charity auction in aid of the Royal Hospital for Sick Children in Edinburgh was to give me a theme of his or her choice for a poem. Having written an extremely generous cheque to the Sick Kids, Gordon W. then asked me for a poem on the theme of 'Everlasting Love', to be dedicated to his wife. Naturally, I was able to draw on my own feelings for my own wife.

How Can the Words *I Love You* . . . ?
(for Susan W. from Gordon W.)

How can the words *I love you* say
what fills my heart? A cliché
cannot cut it. Every day takes on your name;
likewise, the years we've shared, the loving years to come.

How can such a hackneyed phrase express
my feelings? *You* are nothing less
than all my world, the sum
of all my life whose only meaning's this:
your voice, your touch, your kiss.

And so – away with words! Between us two
our every kiss creates our loving world anew.

When the 'creatives' at Irn-Bru started adapting the works
of Rudyard Kipling to help sell their girder-made drink, the
Scotsman *newspaper asked several Scottish writers to revisit*
their own favourite poets. It's always a pleasure to engage with
the sonnet form, even tongue in cheek.

McSonnet

Shall I compare you to a Scottish day?
You are more sunny and less midgey-ridden!
Black clouds may glower until you've had your way,
but then let fall the kisses always hidden

in your smile. Don't laugh – it's true! The mist
that keeps the mountains, glens and lochs from sight
can last for weeks – no promised joys exist
in Scottish rain, no after-storm delight!

Your loving warmth and passion shall not fade
as autumn afternoons, though scarce begun,
turn into winter's chill, for time has made
your touch more intimate and sure – and *fun*!

Evening shadows lengthen, leave no mark,
but our love deepens the nearer comes the dark.

*I never saw a beggar in Edinburgh until Margaret Thatcher's
policies began to grip. Most heartbreaking of all are the homeless
teenagers whose life on the streets, with all its dangers and misery, is
still preferable to whatever life they knew at home.*

Edinburgh is a Thousand Islands

Like you've been travelling in the wrong direction for longer
than you can ever –

Stopping always for good. Always for bad.
A wrecked portacabin, a garage with loose cardboard
        jammed
in the broken window, a builder's skip. Stopping places.
Nothing ever staying the same.
You come back –
the portacabin's gone, the garage window's fixed,
the skip collected.

Edinburgh is a thousand islands – sandstone cliffs, shop
        fronts,
superstores, mini markets, tenements – a thousand islands
with a thousand beaches. Here on the ocean floor –
your blanket, rucksack, plastic cup.

Till everything's closed and shuts you out.

Hauling yourself along the ocean floor
to the nearest shop window. *Discount Furniture.*

Your face, your hair, your fingertips, your breath clouding up,
so much darkness welcoming you among the drowned
and discounted tables, the chairs, sofas and sideboards,
the lamps and ornaments. All there is
is what's traced upon this smoothness of glass.
See-through, see nothing. Break the window
to break into – what?

Days and nights washed up on the Bridges, the Tron steps,
in the Grassmarket, next to ATMs, Pizza Hut,
St James Centre, Argos. Travelling always in the wrong
to the wrong.

A handful of loose change rattles into your cup . . .

Bringing the whole city to a standstill –
Holding back the noise of the sea –

Not managing a word. Not even *Thank you*.

Another morning, another day. Another secret
you'll never share.

No need to struggle to your feet, no need to stand
in front of a shop window –
you already know you're invisible. Daylight *means*
invisibility. When you no longer see yourself, you know
        it's morning.
Cars. Buses. Vans. Taxis. Shoes trampling past –

Invisible. Invisible. Invisible.

More footsteps. Someone slowing down. Stopping.

Are you all right?

A real shit question. Fucker's waiting for an answer,
looking down at you, feeling good and reassured
to know he's not like you.

A real shit question so you want to answer him shit.

Trying to lift up your head, to raise up your eyes.
To look up at his face. To say . . .
To tell him . . .

The words trapped inside you, tearing this way and that,
choking to wrench themselves out.
To spit themselves out.
Words so crammed in your throat they cannot speak –

Staring down at you. Kindness. Concern.
Reaching down to touch you. Your shoulder.
Your hair. You've had those kindnesses before –
you've clawed them and bitten them.

🦢

Cement beach / cement cold / cement hardness . . .

Pretending there's no beach, no islands, no ocean floor,
    no Edinburgh.
Keeping clear of dreams unless they're really happening.
When you wake you're rubbing grit into your face, cutting
glass into your arm.

From a nowhere village in a long-ago countryside of fields
and trees, picture-book farms and rivers.
From a new-town housing scheme.
From Livingston, Glenrothes. From small-town
Dumfries. Peebles. Dunbar. From another planet,
if they want. From Edinburgh itself even.
The countryside, the small town, the city –
what you start saying starts coming true.

Some people need to love too much.
Some people need to hate.

You were abandoned. You were cared for. You were bought
and sold. Lost and found. You ran away.
You're a creature risen from the deep, an angel
fallen from the sky. Whatever.

All you can say . . . is all that you are.

                        ❧

Sitting on the cement beach, trying not to scream.
Shaking with the effort not to.
Shaking, shaking –

Screaming what you can't speak.

Screaming their buses and lorries and cars, their vomit
and dogshit. Screaming their diesel, their dirt,
their concern, their disgust and desire.
Screaming so raw and so loud –
Hauling yourself hand-over-hand out of –
Hauling yourself as far from –

Screaming the daylight that doesn't get through –

Pretending that someone's unexpected kindness –
Pretending someone's hands are steadying you,
their gentleness is steadying you,
holding you. Comforting,
helping the scream sink back inside you.

The secret place inside you is inside them all.
Your secret place. Theirs.
Where everything's gathered close – the kindness,
the cruelty and whatever's left over. Your screams?
You'll nail them to the wall of your secret place.

They're precious. Only you can know how precious they are.

Some mornings I find myself looking out the window of our Newington flat and wondering. Not about the day ahead. Not about life, either. This poem arose from one such moment, leaving me strangely reassured.

Our Piece of Good Fortune

Those of us who've learned to live without drawing breath –

Who start each day falling headlong towards certain
    destruction –

Who darken the clear morning skies like heavier rain –

We've come to grief so often we expect the concrete-slabbed
pavements to flatten us, the streets to run us down,
the empty stretches of the public parks to tidy us from sight,
and the soil of freshly dug gardens to bury us –

but no.

By lunchtime we're out and about, accosting friends and
strangers, telling them how lucky they are,
and how lucky we are.
We're wanting to share our piece of good fortune –
and, after all these years, are still surprised when the likes of
    him, the likes of her
and the likes of them all turn away.

Late afternoon is the worst.
At this low point of the day we try touching base:
What's been achieved? we ask,
looking around us.
And it's too early yet for that first drink of the evening . . .

Soon we're longing for – who knows what?
We're incandescent, you might say.
See us lighting up the night sky – a meteor shower,
falling stars for others to wish upon.
So, go ahead. Why not make a wish?
It seems we've little else to give you.

Those of us who've learned to get through the night
do our best to avoid draughts and awkward furniture in
the dark. When we settle down to sleep we hug
our piece of good fortune to us, as close as we can.

Something to Look Forward to

I know I'll remember this Mallorca moon most of all,
saturating the night sky silver-grey, her light slipping in
and out of my unsteady hands
from how many hundred thousand miles distance?

The sea will remain as calm or as churned-up water;
likewise, the chill transparency of the out-of-season pool,
and these sparrows, hands in their pockets as they
     stand to eat, *peck-*
pecking the white safety rail, drilling for bread;
and the clamour of children and adults, its rise and fall
shredded into momentary sense by my unexpected
understanding of a word, or an intention, as sometimes
happens between us blundering humans.

But this Mediterranean moon's Sea of Tranquillity, her dry
     oceans
and mountain-range silhouettes cut out from warm
     darkness,
will be seen from tomorrow evening onwards
from our top-floor tenement window back in Edinburgh.

A memory is something to look forward to.

The Edinburgh Inspiring Capital *clipper took part in the 2009–10 Clipper Round the World Yacht Race (40,000 miles in total). This poem, written to invoke conditions for a successful voyage, was performed by the crew at the various ports they entered as a sort of calling card. Their first landing was at Rio de Janeiro!*

Incantation for a Good Voyage

Keel, hull, rigging, sail.
Wheel and rudder, mast and muscle,
weather-eye, and skill.

Catch the wind, leave no trail
across the trackless seas.
Balance on air, invisible,

harness hurricane or breeze.
Tilt and tack, swerve and cleave
a path between the unseen

... and the unknown.
Gather squalls and bind
the seven seas.

Leave Edinburgh behind?
No – *we* are its ambassadors,
We *are* our city!

So, steersman, find
safe passage. Let's fill our sails,
set forth for distant shores –

with the Earth itself our steadying keel!

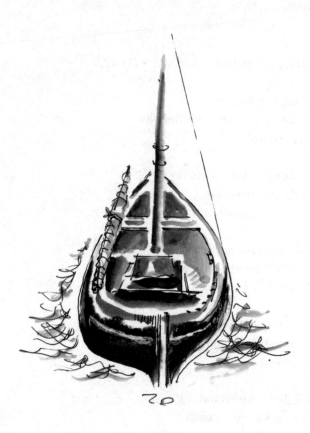

Our City Listens to Itself

The first snowman in the Meadows must have texted his friends.

Schools have locked their doors.
Buses don't know which way to turn, and often don't
mean to. Parked cars become soft furnishings –
a line of them's a scattering of very large pearls threaded
on a string of footprints.
Complete strangers become comrades-in-arms.
'Health and Safety' is sensibly mocked by children
of all ages. Our one and only pet tram's been taken in
out of the cold.

Draped in layer upon layer of near soundlessness,
our city's forced to pause . . . and listen to itself.
Its historic capitalness, its new-found parliamentness,
its always *peopleness*.

We have no one to send into the New Year on our behalf
– and so, until the first snowman volunteers to melt away
into the future, let's make the most of our city
and of ourselves. Let's live for these light-filled days,
this snow-tumbled darkness.

Winter 2010 was fierce. The city was frozen to a standstill. The sub-zero streets resembled a winter scene from Breughel – and yet, there were those who still went around in T-shirts and party skirts!

Going Breughel in Edinburgh

Long trudge the length of Princes Street at two a.m. *Crunch crunch crunching* through driving snow, past waterfalls whose glittering rush has stammered into silence. The east wind's raw. It freeze-dries their lips, razor-cuts their cheeks, sets them stumbling over car-tracks ridged with ice. No traffic, not for hours. So cold, the buildings hold their breath.

T-shirts and jeans, thin dresses and heels, numbed fingers, blurred texts, misspelled greetings, ready to take over the wastelands of after-midnight Lothian Road.

The pizza place and shooter bars have shut early? The lap-dancing club's padlocked? Not even the last remaining bouncer, silver-tinselled and frozen to the spot, can let them in – so they sort him good. Stab him, gut him, trample him, and move on.

Marching into Tollcross grand style, an army of liberation bringing freedom to the arctic streets and shuttered mini-marts. Screaming. Kicking at doors. They're here to make enemies and hunt them down. One of the abandoned cars will do to get them home . . .

(Was that blood they saw spattered in the doorway?
A homeless woman squatting her yellow trickle
in the snow? Who's to say
what five centuries of lacquered-over stillness melt into
in the end – so many lives slipping
through so many fingers . . .)

The long slog across the empty park, Breughel's colours
hardening round them into darkness and chilled stars.
A new moon's cut from purest, near transparent ice.

At Middle Meadow Walk they step into the winter sky –

The Year of the Homecoming was 2009, when Scots from all over the world were encouraged to return to their homeland to visit. Among other events there was a march down the Royal Mile and a massive gathering in Holyrood Park, at which several couples were married.

Homecoming

Internet. Tickets. Suitcase and a plane.
You think it's that easy?
Your passport. Taxi . . . and you're home?

If only.

Nessie, haggis and once-a-year Burns. Sporrans.
Heather. Shortbread tins. Tartan.
Tartan. Tartan. Torness, Faslane,
other people's oil. We're so well-balanced, some of us –
a chip on each shoulder.

This is home? You're welcome.
Living here, we never see our history unless
it's printed on T-shirts, or filmed,
or gift-wrapped.

So, help us. Please.

When you're struggling your suitcases up the Waverley Steps
spare us a thought (you and your return ticket).
Show us what you've come for.

You'll find we're standing on our own two feet,
almost. Walk with us a little.

Show us the way home.

David Hume believed that natural benevolence was a basic human trait – a walk round the city centre usually confirms this. I meet so many people, often complete strangers, who are happy to chat for a few minutes. People like us – 'the understudies for no known part in no known play' – have only got each other for support against those who seem determined to tell us how to live our lives.

The Circle Dante Wasn't Shown

Having reached this stretch of unrecorded ground,
this level stillness of relentless day, we've found
we are alone. Those raising up their hands are branded
by the sun, those falling on their knees in prayer
are kept there. The rest of us trudge forwards – heat
and searing light force us on . . .

Meanwhile: You're waiting for the phone to ring,
waiting for a letter, email, fax, any bloody thing
hinting at reprieve. Each day's a stay of execution:
the stop-and-go of traffic at the lights, the green man, red,
Facebook, Twitter, what the checkout woman said
about the bonus points redemption scheme . . .
You still believe no one's to blame?
When *your* turn comes / your card gets swiped /
you sign your name.

We are the circle Dante wasn't shown:
the understudies for no known part in no known play
– we're waiting to come on
and never will.

Meanwhile: Unpack the Tesco Bag for Life.
Unwrap the pre-cooked chicken, the *no fuss*
prewashed, farmfresh mussels-in-their-shell.

Nearby, in hell, another evening falters to a standstill.

Meanwhile: Fade out the city streets, the sky,
the background music of the spheres –

We'll wait with you till everything around you disappears:
wait upon this stretch of unrecorded –
this level stillness of –
this heat and
searing
light

Jack Vettriano's painting The Singing Butler *is iconic. It also inspired a play by Alexis Zegerman that was broadcast on BBC Radio 4 (17 May 2007). Having been asked to write a poem to be inserted between scenes, I imagined my painter remembering a childhood experience at Gullane, just along the coast from Edinburgh. Unfortunately I've never had the opportunity to ask Mr Vettriano if he's ever been there, nor if his creative process bears any resemblance to what follows . . .*

The Singing Butler

PART ONE

Standing in T-shirt and jeans spattered red, yellow and blue –

Empty studio, easel, rainbow-smeared palette, sunlight
slanting through uncurtained glass –
Paintings already finished and already stacked
against the wall . . . Dead things.

Always the same headlong fall into
silence? Emptiness? Yourself?

Don't try to hold on.
Don't try.
Remember when you were a child and *tried* to get to sleep –
it was the very act of *trying* stopped you.
Natural as breathing, dreaming.

Except for the scent of . . . ?
Except for the very faintest . . .?

Don't try to understand it, to force it, to grab hold –
let it gradually . . . imperceptibly . . .
A scent of something long ago.
Something faraway in time, in place –
A time of day that doesn't happen to you any more,
a place that's elsewhere now. But so familiar.

The white plaster walls and wooden floor of your studio fading,
drifting out of reach.
                    And in their place –
                              this scent . . .
                                        this smell of open air!
Wind blowing as from another world. A cold wind.
A cold sea-wind carrying salt-tang, freshness.

Too soon yet for the canvas, the brushes and paint.
Too soon for you to make your mark. Relax.
You're *there*.
Walking out of Gullane, across the sloping stretch of grass,
the neat-and-tidy park, the criss-crossed green, the worn-down
brown, the path you're running on.
You're carrying the dozen-times-a-year bucket and
spade, the towel and trunks.
Your parents following with the picnic food, the tea and lemonade.
A day out. A holiday.
A getting-away-from-it-all day!

How you run and run ahead of them to reach that
in-the-distance sea-blue turning
into sky-blue!
Coarse grass slashing at your bare legs,
sea air cutting clean!
Kick off your sandals. The hard ground's gone so crumble-soft
your pounding, run-fast feet feel
shifting sand beneath them,
feel loose, slowing-you-down, slithering sand beneath them . . .

Don't try to remember . . . Don't try to force . . .

Untimely darkness spills across the sky.

Distant glittering blue turns metal-grey,
the wet sand fades to washed-out –

The sea is dying; the sky's its shroud.

Inside you, something's just about to change . . .

🕊

Look at the palette with your innermost eye:
that blue *is* a stretch of clearest blue sky,
and that isn't yellow, or green or grey
but smears of cloud, a tumbling spray
of seawater . . .

Let the sweep of your brush
upon canvas reveal what's hidden inside.
Dead paint becomes colour, *live* colour – the rush
of the wind, the run of the tide.

Squeeze out the blue, squeeze out the sky!
Squeeze out the red, and the sun's set high!
Brush-stroke brown puts the beach in place,
a dark yellow smudge for someone's face.

The day's work is done, the job well begun,
the canvas is no longer bare.
there's a hint of a scene, and what it might mean
– on that six-year-old day you were there.

How you ran and you ran down the slope to the sand,
the sea stretching far, far away!
Well, that sea is in you, your childhood is too –
still happening now, and today.

That shifting sand, that darkening sky.
The child and the man – one will live,
one will die?

PART TWO

Eight o'clock – in bed.

Nine o'clock – in bed.

Tired body, tired head.

Ten o'clock. Up. Dressed.
Coffee, coffee, coffee's best.

You're feeling better with every sip.
The kitchen feels better with every sip.
The world feels better with every sip.
Another cup and you're ready to grip
a paintbrush, ready to dip
its tip into the past –

A woman in a red dress, and a man.
You're running down the path too fast –
You see them. Trip.

They're holding hands, they kiss.

You scramble to your feet. Too young to be discreet,
you stand and watch,
watch them hold hands, watch them kiss.

The sun clouds over –
the chill's abrupt. The lovers shiver,
holding each other tighter. And *this* –
this holding tight, this shivering kiss –
marks when all your histories must start,
your histories and your art.

A shout! He's seen you, he starts to yell
telling you to get the hell
away from them. Picking up
his girlfriend's parasol like it was a stick
to beat you with. He's twice your size, or even more!
He's rushing over . . .
                              Double-quick,
and from a standing start, you run faster
than you've ever run before!

Are you running still? Not a blue sky anymore, but grey.
Exactly like it turned that day.
No more sea-glittering ultramarine,
but ditchwater green – an oil-sheen
transparency that breaks upon discoloured sand.

Cloud, wind and rain.
An ebb-tide scene of desolation . . .

Desolation you cannot understand.

PART THREE

That couple holding hands, you paint them centre stage.
You paint them dancing in the storm: 'Let it rage!'
they say, 'for we're together
whatever the weather!'
they say, as they sway
to music only they
can hear . . .

You stop. You're done, or think you are –
as if paint was merely meant for painting-over,
making real things disappear.

It's a child's-eye view you give us of the scene –
this couple dancing carelessly between
the hectic colours spattered on the beach. This is joy?
Spontaneous affection? Love? The small boy
who stood and watched can stand and watch no longer.
The adult world with all its threatening weather,
comes too soon – it always comes too soon. Is this why
you watch your hand now take the brush and try
to intervene . . .
to paint in what had *never* been?

Here a dab of white . . .
                    some grey . . .
                              the beginnings of a line . . .
Don't think. Don't try to understand – just *paint*!
A smudge . . .
          another smudge . . .
                              a very faint
                    suggestion of a figure.
    Two figures now emerging out of –
More paint –
              another man and woman, standing by,
not dancing, and not in love.
They're wet, they're cold. They try
to hold this picture of romance together, to protect

the carefree innocents, before their loving world is
    wrecked.

Guardian angels? Sort of. These are servants placed
between love's innocence and the storm –
not with parasols, but umbrellas raised up high
like good intentions. The maid's afraid her cap will fly
off in the wind . . . she didn't ask to be here,
but here she is. Like the best and worst of us, she's learnt
to bear the role she's stuck with. Not so
the butler. Again the brush, you watch it go
onto the palette, load up on black,
turn the dancing floor to black,
the strip of sky to black.
That's the butler, exhausted, sagging at the knees.
No wonder, since his childhood he has sought to please,
to stand, to look on while other people live.

But now – your masterstroke! You give
this painted scene its heart,
the touch of human warmth that raises art
above the commonplace. You call your work
The Singing Butler. His unheard voice is bringing
music to the dancing couple, to their imaginary ball,
and carries them above the storm –
its soundless echo ringing deep within us all.

Music Edinburgh

Contemporary Music in Scotland

In the absence of an orchestra in his muddy Scottish village
the boy conducts the trees, his string section. Gradually
the cattle on the hillside, the birds, the wind, the river,
the farmer's dog, the sound of rain – everything seen
and unseen is given its place on his unwritten score.

At school he has the finger pointed at him. The teacher,
a firm believer in Scottish Education, stands him out in front
to conduct the morning's noise.
He'll be kept there till he's learned his lesson –
enough tears, and a sneer will pass for kindness,
red hair turn to flame.

The houses here are made from the ruins of other houses,
from the rubble and brickwork of the castle.
The mad are penned together near the flooded field;
the others buy and sell daylight, trading colour
for colour. Dusk alone brings close of business.

The fire burns low. He stares into a darkness silvered here and
    there
by stars and transatlantic flight paths. He cannot sleep for
    listening
to the restless hills and streams, to their unplayed music,
to the wayward moon soundlessly turning
on its invisible rope.

Edward Harper (1941–2009) was one of this country's major composers, particularly of opera. He lived in Edinburgh for many years and lectured in composition at the university. I had the honour to provide texts for two of his symphonies, which involved most enjoyable discussions fuelled by wine and real ale. His last few years were a battle against cancer. He was a lovely man and is sorely missed.

Haydn and Chemotherapy

How many weeks since we were last together –
five? Six? At our age, time passes quicker,
so they tell us.

A Sunday afternoon. We shared a meal, some wine,
we chatted about Haydn and chemotherapy.
You said you felt a little tired,
and afterwards lay down.

We left you outside, standing at your gate –
so many days and weeks remained to struggle through:
Vienna one last time, the *Krankenhaus*, more drugs, more
        tests,
working on your symphony. You waited, hand
resting on the latch, to give us all a wave.

Another Sunday at your house.
We sit together, your family and mine. We're trapped
at this still point – around us, Time's onward rush sends
the clock hands wheeling madly round the hours
to come, as though searching for you.

The next minute, the next second, the next heartbeat –
we *must* live through them. Only then
will we feel your touch and hear your voice,
and once more see you wave goodbye.

In 2002, news reports told how the family of a Jewish student from Glasgow, killed by a Palestinian suicide bomber while visiting Tel Aviv, donated his organs to save the life of a Palestinian girl. Two years later, in a separate incident, a twelve-year-old Palestinian boy was shot dead by an Israeli soldier while playing with a toy gun. In an act of astonishing generosity, his family donated his organs to a number of beneficiaries, including two Israeli children. This was Edward Harper's starting point for his Second Symphony *– and he asked me to provide a text based on these events.*

The Time for Miracles
(for baritone, choir and orchestra)

Them! Them! Them!
Not me! Not you! Not us!
THEM! THEM! THEM!
Not us! Not us! Not us!

Who are they?

Not us! Not us! Not us!

Who are we?

The First! The Best!

Who are they?

The Worst! The Cursed!

Their skin, their eyes, their hatred, their lies.
Our eyes, our skin, our love, our truth.
Killing them, we love our own.

❧

My son Ahmed – his eyes, his skin.
His twelve years.
My son Ahmed playing the game he saw around him.
His plastic gun. The soldiers.
My son Ahmed – shot where he played.
All his years to come –
All his unborn children's lives to come –
Stopped. Dead.

We cannot raise the dead.
Cannot return the bullet to the gun,
the gun to the holster.

Nor hatred to the poisoned heart.

We cannot begin again. History has no full stops,

only each child's birth and death. So many children.

So many heartbeats flicker on the monitors –

Arab/Jewish monitors. Arab/Jewish heartbeats.
Listen to the heartbeats.
Listen to the silence between the heartbeats . . .

That silence where terror begins.
Yours / Mine. Theirs / Ours.

❧

Let us step across this silence,

Let us reach across the terror.

Now is the time for miracles:
the gift of Jewish life to Arab,
the gift of Arab life to Jew.
Now – or Time itself will stop.

Out of death, let there come life.
Out of hatred, let there come acceptance.

Let our gifts raise us all from the dead –
you and me, them and us.

We are the living, we are our only hope.

Three Composers Respond to the Politics of Perpetual War

Having worked extensively with Edinburgh-based composers for many years on operas, symphonies and song cycles, I sometime find myself wondering about composer-magicians elsewhere. Here are three who, though no longer with us, are still regarded as very contemporary.

In the 1920s, Arnold Schoenberg developed his twelve-tone technique of composition, which contributed hugely to the move away from tonal music. Not everybody loved the sounds he made, but the world itself was going through some very unlovely experiences at that time.

1. How Schoenberg's Twelve-tone Technique Might Have Led to a Better World, but Didn't

Like everyone else at the end of the nineteenth century,
Arnold Schoenberg had taken his seat on the crowded train
heading towardsan ever-better world.
As it turned the corner into the glorious future ahead,
the engine started picking up speed –
moments later slamming into a solid wall.

Bits went everywhere: bits of countries, bits of colonies,
bits of science, art and religion.
The tracks, seeming to stretch back to the beginnings of
Time, were wrenched apart;
buckled and bent, they clawed at the blue sky
above Passchendaele.

Suddenly the street was full of people who knew best.
Their self-appointed task:
to get civilisation back on the rails.
They all agreed that drastic problems need
        drastic solutions –
and each had a solution more drastic than the one before.

Such a noise of hammering and welding!
Such a clamour and din of revolution, extermination,
colonial expansion and unemployment,
of mass production and racial purity!
The Stock Exchange boomed, the trains ran on time.

Schoenberg, meanwhile, had discarded tonality, declaring
his twelve-tone system would create a melodic line strong
enough to hold everything together.
Even Chaos itself.

Around him, the street was bustling with strikers and strike-
breakers, with cattle trucks criss-crossing Europe,
financiers thudding onto pavements, parades,
searchlights, flags, roaring ovens,

transatlantic crossings to the sounds of the restaurant
orchestra, reasoned debate and orderly soup queues.

Soon Schoenberg was rushing up to complete strangers –
My twelve-tone system offers real value for money to composer,
player and audience alike.

Darkness fell swifter than ever before. Once the lights
    went out,
The Sandman tiptoed from country to country, tucking
the sleepers tight in their beds.

That done, he began telling them their dreams.

The composer John Cage was a great believer in pure chance and wished to eliminate not only the personal, but also the human element from many of his compositions. Interesting as an idea, perhaps?

2. Between Hollywood Immortality and Life and Death on Wall Street: The Earliest Days of John Cage

The third day in Cage's life began before
the second had finished. Counterpoint of a sort,
he remarked to himself while watching a half-
completed dream get spiked onto the city skyline.

For the next week his nursery was ransacked
by the impatient future. Teddy's glass eye winked
at shutter-speed: record-erase / record-erase /
record-erase . . . Deformed as we all are
by our longings, Cage wept childish tears
for the rest of his life. As we all do.

He knew, when aged a fortnight, that he already knew
     too much –
The city skyline, that bundle of *I Ching* sticks, was ready
     to be thrown –
America, that blood-red carpet laid down to welcome
the twentieth century, fitted perfectly
(it was the world, of course, that needed trimmed).

The future was always one step ahead –
a part-developed print, a ghost
that left tracks.

Let's pretend, he said to himself while clutching
the playpen bars that kept him safer than love,
let's pretend the West Coast and the East (Hollywood
immortality, life and death on Wall Street)
are lines drawn in the desert: traced out
and erased / traced out and
erased / traced out and erased . . .

The sands of Time, the arithmetic of Chance.

The Desert of New Mexico:
The Manhattan Project + Los Alamos = Hiroshima
The Desert of Nevada:
Las Vegas + this (for-one-lifetime-only) 4-dimensional dice
= our aging towards a certainty.

Meanwhile from the sand grain's empty heart, from its
    lifeless core –

Silence / Silence / Silence

Karlheinz Stockhausen was best known for his electronic and orchestral compositions, many of which are extremely lengthy. Extremely self-indulgent too, say some. His written texts make for fascinating reading, not least for the claim that his music was created for the post-Apocalypse era. He is on record saying that he came from a planet in the Sirius system and would return there when his work on Earth was done.

3. Stockhausen's Soundtrack for the post-Apocalpyse Will Be Written in Strict Symphonic Form

1. Allegro Perpetuo

Cut and loop the TV clips to send that second plane
into that second tower inside our head. Now every plane
in every empty sky blazes into red
and yellow flames inside our head.

And so –

Cut and loop the TV clips . . .

2. Adagio

Five billion dollars' darkness glides five miles above:
no stain across the radar sky, no sonic boom disturbing us
five miles below. No unnecessary din.

We're free to look on while our town, our street,
our work-place and our homes are re-designed
with state-of-the-art efficiency –

our grandparents, children, husbands, wives, cousins
friends, arms, legs, eyes, hands, skin.

3. Scherzo and Trio

Switch off the moon, turn up the sun,
Stockhausen's soundtrack has begun.

New York and Kabul are suburbs of the same world.
Cluster bombs and food parcels drop
from the same planes.
Cancel the earth, delete the stars,
Stockhausen's soundtrack will do for all wars.

4. Allegro

That clear September morning in Manhattan.
The night-sky above the Afghan desert, above Baghdad.
We turn from one to see the other. There's nothing else.
Stockhausen's soundtrack. Then end-of-tape *hiss* . . .

Cassandra was granted the gift of prophecy by Apollo, but was also doomed never to be believed. She was a captive, a trophy slave forced to live in exile, and could be seen as the ultimate victim. The Edinburgh-based composer Lyell Cresswell, set these poems for his large-scale oratorio about exile, Shadows Without Sun. *The king and queen are Agamemnon and Clytemnestra.*

Two of Cassandra's Songs

1. CASSANDRA'S LAMENT

What I see is what I say –
five continents of sense becoming one.
My own, this sixth sense. Mine alone.
Shadows without sun, their every touch contagion –
some chill, some burn.
Only the scars are mine –
invisible as loss, or hope.

2. CASSANDRA'S GIFTS

For the king: a crown of iron and splintered bone.
For the queen: a robe of spattered blood.

My gifts for my royal masters.
To curse them. To call them to their time.

The rest, the undisclosed, is mine –
slavery, exile and the blessings of the unforeseen.

Commissioned to write a Concerto for Voice and Violin by the BBC for their Festival of the Violin, Lyell Cresswell asked me to provide a text to celebrate this wonderful instrument. This piece – and hauntingly beautiful it is, too – was recorded for Naxos. Lyell is a good friend and great company – hence the playfulness of some of the movements!

The Voice Inside

I. LARGO

Hush . . . Hush . . .
 Hush the strings . . .
 Hush the body . . .
 Still the bow to silence echoing
 the silence long before
 the strings, the body
and the bow.
Before the strings were laid in place,
pegged and tied, stretched and
tightened taut.
Before arching them into the emptiness all around,
holding the greater silence echoing
the greatest silence
ever.

Then touch –
 Hush –
 Touch –
 Hush –

Touch . . . Stroke to sound . . .
Draw sound out of tightness,
                              out of stillness,
                                        out of emptiness . . .
          Shaping the emptiness that everything
     comes from and returns to.
Giving it scale –
          Giving it voice –
                    Giving it life.

2. SCHERZO I: DUET

Your voice / My voice
Sound plaited with sound.
Silence layered upon silence –
criss-crossing, parting,
sliding together
to harmonise,
to kiss.

And O, those fugal lines
of tig and catch,
               touch and snatch,
     tag and miss.
Catch as catch can –
boy and girl / woman, man.

Your theme or mine?

Line for line, into the bars –
and out.

Your key or mine?
– let's intertwine!

3. VIGOROUS

Not a woman's voice – NO.
Hard and harshness
Stride and strident.

Not a woman's voice – NO.
Slash / strike / cut / score.

Not pleading, not pleasing, not –

Wound to the heart.
Stab to the soul.

Scar / scrape / mark / march

Destroy. Destroy. Destroy.

4. SLOW MOVEMENT

Sound has always held itself as absence
in the slackened strings, in the hollowed body,
in the unstrung bow.
As presence – the soul as silence.

5. SCHERZO 2

Four strings, body and bow.
Locatelli, Corelli,
Paganini, Tartini,
Neil Gow! Neil Gow! Neil Gow!

Four strings, body and bow.
Guarneri, Amati,
Stradivari, Viotti,
Vivaldi, Grapelli,
Spohr, Spivakovsky,
Neil Gow! Neil Gow! Neil Gow!

6. BURLESQUE

Twelve equal tones dangling on a score,
if one of them should modulate,
would there be a melody
where none had been before?

Twelve equal tones dangling on a stave,
if all of them should modulate,
which one would we save?

Chaos comes but once a year,
Creation's always late –
so choose the note you like to hear,
the rest will sublimate!

7. PLEA

Hear my voice, hear me listening to
the voice inside, the voice
so deep, deep inside –

Rising up from the core of the earth it feels,
from the furthest rim of the farthest star it feels,
from the darkest hour, the darkest night,
the radiant sun at noon –
into my heart, into my lungs, my throat.

Revealing what I do not know.

Expressing what I dare not feel.

Saying what cannot keep silent.

Virtual Edinburgh

The Other Edinburgh

Sometimes Princes Street enjoys having a good long stretch
before settling down for the night.
The Scott Monument yawns, setting off Jenners,
the Balmoral . . . Rose Street doesn't want to go home yet,
but then it never does. At Waverley, the trains sag on their
axles, their carriages gathering darkness to fill
the empty hours ahead.

Three floors up our Newington tenement we hear
the street door slam
shut – that's Dod come home. Beanie, boots, vodka,
sleeping bag. After the stairwell allows itself one last turn
to get more comfortable, the flats begin slowly
tipping us over an edge we didn't
even know was –

This other city's history is our own. Its pitch-black vennels,
vaults, closes, wynds piled each on each
and in perpetual free-fall – these are the nights
we live through, set in stone.

When our time comes, shall we find ourselves washed up one
by one on an elsewhere shore? A very Scottish baptism.
So far north what else is there to live for, excepting kindness
– kindness and hoarded daylight?

The same repeated streets, the same clumsiness of hopes
     and fears –
this is our only destination, our only journey.

This is the once-in-a-lifetime of it all.

David Hume (1711–1776) was one of the greatest philosophers ever.
He doubted everything, his own existence and all religion included.
An endless stream of local divines turned up at his deathbed urging
him to accept God. He thanked them for their concern – and refused.
By all accounts, he passed away quite at his ease.

David Hume Takes a Last Walk on Arthur's Seat

Not bothering to set his alarm clock, David Hume
took to his deathbed.
He lay down, got himself comfortable and closed his eyes.
On this most special occasion, he pictured a real summer's
afternoon smelling of heather, sun-warmed rocks,
a hint of sea air blowing in from the Forth.
At peace, he let the grass and whins of Arthur's Seat come
sloping down to welcome him.

Just then an untidy-looking sheep glanced up, interrupting
its day-long meal. It stared at him.
What happens now? asked the dying man. The sheep stood its
ground, blinked. Stopped chewing.
Well? prompted the sceptic's sceptic, whose studies had
     reinforced
his belief that in such matters we each need
all the help we can get.

The lightly sketched-in clouds were stationary. The sun
stood still for the first time since
that ancient god had stopped it briefly
in its tracks, in the name of love.

The sheep strolled over. It coughed, and was about to
    speak when –

Visitors. Bloody visitors. Hume could hear them barging
    in through his front door,
cluttering up his hallway with their endless taking off of
    hats and wigs,
their loud disrobing of noisy raincoats, their pulling off
    of sopping-wet summer galoshes.
Their standing around discussing him in whispers.

Meanwhile his perfect afternoon was heading nowhere –
the sheep had thinned down to a dwindling hank
of scrag-wool on sticks, the clouds condensing into
raindrops that would never fall,
the hillside's green and broom-yellow dissolving into
ever-weakening sunlight.
Here and there, his bedroom furniture was already
showing through.

Uninvited callers! Comforting words! Concern for his
    mortal soul!

He fights back. Eyes firmly closed to blot out this micro-flock
of Scottish ministers determined on his salvation,
Hume returns to Arthur's Seat. He repositions the sun
and sets it moving across the sky once more;
he restores the nearest clouds as best he can,
fills in enough of the path to let him walk in safety.

Come nightfall, he's reached the summit. Edinburgh lies
spread out far below.

He takes his first step into utter and perpetual darkness –
and the darkness holds.

Another step. And then another.

Soon he's walking directly above the city. Unnamed stars and
undiscovered galaxies congregate around him.
He knows each step could be his last. *As in life*,
he whispers, *so let it be in death*.

And smiling to himself alone, he puts his best foot forward.

David Hume applied to teach philosophy at Edinburgh University, and was turned down. In the 1960s the new tower block housing the philosophy department was named after him. This poem was commissioned to celebrate the 75th anniversary of the Saltire Society.

David Hume's History of Scottish Weather

Sittin in the Chair of Philosophy the uni willnae gie him,
halfweys up the Tower they hivnae yet named efter him,
Hume rubs at the windae. 'Is there ocht oot there
barrin Scotch mist?' He rubs an he rubs
at the clairt o history smirran up the gless wi bad bluid,
battles an betrayals: 'Does Scottish daylight even
ken tae struggle through?'

Eleven hunner year almaist tae the day whaun Oingus
    saw
the blue sky an white cloud cross o victory, the Saltire
Society comes intae its ain. McDiarmid, Muir an ithers
step up tae tak their turn. They rub an they rub –
an throu the porridge-coloured stour mak oot a country,
but only just, an a culture held th'gither yince a year
by servin up the National Bard as trimmings tae a haggis.

The weather warsens. Fair drookit, Scottish heroes
get stunted peerie-weerie doun tae wee bit laddies
– Peter Pan, Wee McGreegor, Oor Wullie.
No a grown man amangst them. Weans
wi a Westminster faither ...

Seventy-five year on, a keek o sunlicht's warmin up the gless
(*Scottish* sun, that is). Devolution's turned us adolescent
– grown-up, but no quite. Pocket money,
but nae income. No politics, mair an attitude.
We're thrang at Hume's historic windae, rubbin
at the gless like spey-wives at their crystal baas. 'Whit's
the weather up tae? Whit wey's the wund blaain nou?'

Whae says he kens oor future, is nocht but faain
fer a trick o the licht, he's self-deceivin
at best – we canna leave oor country's politics
tae pairty-politicians, oor culture tae moose-click
          bureaucrats.
It's time tae thraw Hume's windae – thon keekin-gless
o guid intentions – wide, wide open, reclaim the present.
Best fit forrad, heel-an-toe!

Hume's aye wi us, MacDiarmid, Muir an aa the laive
are at oor side, the blue and white's abune. But mind,
the Saltire's no a comfort blanket,
a patterned plaid tae wrap oorsels in, snod
an bien, an keep oor sweet dreams sweet
– thon's a windin sheet!
Insteid, spreed oot, it's muckle sail eneuch an strang
tae catch aa Scottish weathers – and hurl us alang!

The National Monument on Calton Hill was built to commemorate
those killed in the Napoleonic Wars. Designed in imitation of the
Parthenon, it was begun in 1826 and abandoned unfinished when
the money ran out. Sometimes, however, ghosts have other plans . . .

The Completed Parthenon
on Calton Hill

Toiling along Princes Street, then up Waterloo Place,
a Doric pillar on each shoulder. Victorious, immortal –
us and our classically proportioned back-breaking loads.

We left our dead on the battlefield – they're always allowed for
in advance, calculated like futures, hedge funds,
algorithms of acceptable loss.

Everyone's conscience is clear, and when the sums don't
work out no one's to blame
but history.

Two centuries on, we've slowed to a standstill almost –
nothing more than a trick of the light,
our exhaustion the wind sighing high above the city.

The completed Parthenon is all that matters. We'll get there.
One day we'll slot the missing pillars in, cement them,
stick on a roof, a frieze.

Until then we only need keep going.

Below us, the spread-out streets and shopping malls
    surge electric,
what's human soon delivers up its soul.

Whoever wanders here, take care. These unfinished
stones mark unfinished wars – as all wars are.

The Juggler of Greyfriars Kirkyard

Having set the rush of particles imprisoned within the stone
wall spinning in unlikely orbits, the juggler steps through
newly created Space –
to stand upon the kirkyard grass.

His fingers seize the winter sunlight; he'll hone its edge
upon the sorrowing and almost-toppled-over headstones,
he'll scrape clear any loving words weathered
down to whispers.

A mausoleum slab to someone's dearly departed,
disfigured angels, doves, slime-green weeping maidens
and their urns . . . whatever he touches he raises up

to weightlessness. Tossing them from hand to hand, he feels
for hidden gravities – the trapped pulse, the heartbeat
buried at the granite's core.

One by one he gets them on the move, and soon they're
tumbling faster and faster round him –

Then, his grand finale, he hurls them far into the sky
to find a resting place among the stars . . .

Performance over, he takes his bow, withdraws.
Meanwhile the particles resume familiar orbits, to wall
    him in once more
within infinities of stone and loss.

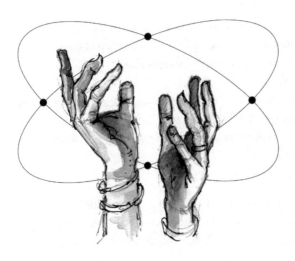

To the north of Princes Street is the New Town, an area of Georgian houses laid out in elegant crescents, streets and lanes. Home to some of Edinburgh's bankers and lawyers, it has gained a reputation for solid wealth and polite society. But when left to its own devices . . . ?

The New Town's Response to the Threat of Global Warming

New Towners, so rumour has it, love to hopscotch
their northern cobbles, go line-dancing up and
down their choreography of crescents,
their solemnity of squares.
With acres of well-dressed stone and highly polished sunlight
as a playground, few waste time in basement-
below-basement vaults of damp and stagnant wealth.

Instead . . .

The instant the likes of you and me have gone back
to where we came from, the hula-hoops come out!
There's lunchtime kick-the-can and rounders, after-hours
     sardines,
flap-the-kipper all night, every night.
The PRIVATE on their tight-
shut, fiercely locked-up gardens means
they're on their pogo-sticks or playing hide-and-seek.
They live for weekend tournaments of squeak,
piggie, squeak!

One day a trampolining banker bounced – *boing!*
back down to earth. He had been – *boing!* – launched
an hour before, but now – *boing!* – (public-school
complexion blanched)
boing! – he'd had enough. 'I've bounced so high
I've seen – *boing!*–
the future:

the hurricanes and palm trees,
the homeless polar bears,
the penguins, iguanas
marching here in pairs.
McDonald meat on dust plains,
no pollen and no bees,
melting ice-caps, dinosaurs
out from their deep freeze.
Where's Noah when you need him?
Who's bailing out the seas?

Logos, no-goes, tariffs, terror,
cyber-sex and crazy weather!
Cashback. Points earned. Server glitch.
Mega-poor and mega-rich.
Credit rating. Credit crunch.
Decaf coffee, wineless lunch.
Virus. Trojan. Password. PIN.
Can't log out / Can't log in . . .'

'Calm down . . . Don't panic any more . . .
you're back on solid ground –
richer even than before:
we'll profit from the falling pound.

Mother Nature will take care
we don't come to disaster.
Rising seas and temperatures?
Inflation's rising faster!

Make your hard cash sweat.
Get flexible. Get lean –
and then restructured, re-financed,
get back upon that trampoline!'

EPILOGUE: (Please choose from menu below)

Option 1
The banker listened, was inspired.
He bought and sold the world, and then retired.
Liquidation to the nearest million pound
brought happiness, till he was found
floating on his sea of money
– drowned!

Option 2

The banker listened, but declined. He gave his share
to Greenpeace. Took up trampolining full-time where
he died contented – in mid-air!

Option 3

The banker played the market, never stopped.
Trampolined in sun and rain. On he hopped –
'This time I'll bring us back a shining star
to light up every New Town street and lane!'
Alas, he boinged a *boing!* too far
– and was never seen again!

The rewiring and replumbing of our Newington flat felt like an invasion
as we tried and failed to enjoy normal family life. Everyday life in a
country where others seem to have more and more power over our personal
decisions feels similarly invaded.

Somewhere in these Sky-Blue Streets

The afternoon sky's flooding our Edinburgh streets summer-blue?

We're walking as through a light-drenched forest laden with azure
    fruit?

Sleepwalking, more like.

Meanwhile someone's pressed down hard on our spinning world,
and stilled it. There's an action plan,
bullet points to asset-strip our lives.
Can't you hear their finger *tap-tap-tapping* the surface
of the earth to help us keep in step,
keep us marching in the right direction?

Did we ask for this army of liberation to occupy our flat?
Financial meltdown in the front room?
Our kitchen forcibly upgraded to a parliament where morality's
the small print no one reads?

Of course we didn't.

But somewhere in these sky-blue streets,
in the unsounded oceans of the public squares and gardens,
the dream we've stumbled into is not our own.
Not any more.

                        ❧

Delete the permanence of stone cemented onto stone.
Refresh each rush of multi-coloured pixels on the screen.

From time to time we remember we're at war,
remember the street we live in *is* the front line.

We're in a dream within a dream, wandering
from one into the next. Cities blister in the unprotected sun.

Make peace with the gods of earth and sky?
or with each other?

Transport initiatives are currently all the rage in Edinburgh, in every sense of the word. In an effort to calm the civic breast, here is a modest suggestion.

The Gondolas of South Bridge

Trapped by a Scottish downpour that's already lasted
    centuries,
we're outside Poundstretcher, stuck in the bus shelter.
Here the heavens can fall only so far, pooling
into the shallow metal lake inches above our head.
We wait, and dream of gondolas.

– *Some rain, eh?* says one man, gazing upstream to Surgeon's
    Hall
and downstream to the Tron.
– *Call this rain?* Says another, gobbing into the flood
(he's ankle-deep and loving it).
*The cistern that was flushed empty long, long ago
is only now starting to re-fill. Soon the Castle'll have a moat,
tides'll break upon the shores of Princes Street,
developing a taste for plate-glass windows
and Georgian stonework.*

– *These gondolas?* A woman asks.
– *Aye?*
– *A new transport initiative? An integrated system with the buses,
    so that –?*
– *Ye've seen yer last bus.*

– With the trams then, so that –?
– Trams! (another gob mightier than the last) *Gon-dol-as,*
    I'm telling you!
Our only hope in this damn climate. Fleets of them,
flotillas, convoys lining up along the City Bypass.
We'll hear them serenading nearer when the time comes.
– And the rain?
– Ye call this rain?

Meanwhile our city drowns – an underwater gridlock of
    good intentions stalled,
rusting to a standstill.
There's rumour of a Works Department plug that might
    get pulled.

Like it or not, we were all born yesterday.
Who can tell what this deluge means to the clans of
    Scottish fish
patrolling their puddled wee lochan above?
Theirs is a soundless ceilidh.

When the waters rise enough to flood them out, will they
    glide off
with a tartan flick of the tail to swim the Gardens,
the New Town, Leith and out to sea –

leaving us to develop gills ourselves?

The quite magnificent statue of Sir Walter Scott (1771–1832) sits within the base of the Scott Monument in Princes Street. As well as being Scotland's best-known literary figure, Scott was also a man of strong political convictions. He is reputed to have wept publicly on the Mound when he heard about the passing of the Great Reform Act enfranchising the majority of the British population. I wonder what he would have made of Scotland's new parliament.

A Day in the Afterlife of Sir Walter Scott

After 150 years of doing nothing, thinking nothing, staring
     at nothing
and looking as if he *might* have something on his mind –
Sir Walter Scott decided that enough
was enough. Indeed, it was more than enough.

Being twice life-size and head-to-toe Carrara marble surely
counted for something these days – no?

So he sat in his monument, and he planned. A few more years
     passed.

Right! he said one morning.

Another year passed.

Right! he said again and stood up. Intended to, at least . . .
Didn't quite manage. And so, putting every ounce of will-
     power

into every pound of solid marble, he tried again to draw
     himself slowly and
painfully up to his full height.

For the first time in over 150 years, Sir Walter Scott was
     back on his feet!

Young David Young, a truant from the edge of town,
happened to be passing:
'Who're you?'

Sir Walter knew the answer, but was well aware that more
     urgent problems
confronted the country of his birth. Harnessing the full
     power
of his mighty frame, he manoeuvred himself round
to face the Balmoral Hotel, and began
the laborious journey to
HOLYROOD!

֍

'I am a Baronet – where is the Upper House?'

'Need to scan you, sir. Also, there's Health and Safety.
To get you through the parliamentary doorways, along
the parliamentary corridors,
up and down the parliamentary stairs –

you'll need to lose some marble.
Legs or head?'

By lunchtime, Sir Walter had returned to his monument,
      muttering to himself –
'In the Good Old Days . . . all but single-handedly . . .
Scotland's vision of itself . . . its literature, its history.'

Well he *had*, hadn't he?

No one saw his tears this time – because there were none.
No one saw him beating his marble head against the arching
stone that rose above his marble chair – because he didn't.

Instead –

and just as the One o'Clock Gun went off –

he took his seat once more,
resumed his pose of tireless immortality.

'Way to go, Big Man!' Young David Young welcomed him
      back.
'WAY TO GO!'

A Proposal for Our City's Digital Upgrade

(The proposed virtual river will flow the length of Princes Street
Gardens following the railway tracks, from Waverley to the West
End – *and no further*. The Council considers this adequate for
something that's invisible.)

The winter homepage will link to a pre-global warming app.
We'll Hogmanay Party Siberian-style, complete with samovars,
sleighs and Cossack-dancing on the frozen ice.
At twelve, we'll listen for the New Year bells across the centuries
of falling snow, prepared at last to bare our Scottish souls
– those sub-zero lumps of natural benevolence will do
to keep the vodka chilled.

(Those who fish for underwater trains will require a licence to
hook, net, gut *and* grill – in designated areas *only*.
A second licence will allow their sale by length and destination.)

🦢

Spring's screensaver will show Seurat's *Bathing at Asnières*.
And so, knowing the horrors soon to come, we'll Delete the
    twentieth century,
Cut and Paste a reformatted menu – 'Options We Can Live With'.
Then press Select/ Select/
Select until we get the future right.

(A third licence will be required by those who wish to lever
open carriage roofs, searching for pearls.)

·❧·

On shirt-sleeved summer evenings the Ganges will be our
        homepage.
Sluggish with brown mud, clotted with cremation ash, with
        holy men
and more gods than even the reincarnated have time for,
this holy river will seem to flood the Gardens.
Tourists will edge away in case the hat comes round,
but we'll just shrug and blame it on the trams.

(Should inner-city baptisms prove popular, Health & Safety
have decreed the *baptee* shall be led down a flight of virtual
steps cut into the riverbank at the point where the train lines
entering Waverley are seen to fan out into a slower-flowing
delta – and *nowhere else*.
Total immersions will be instantly uploaded onto YouTube.
Motto – if the moment's saved . . . then so are you.)

·❧·

Post-Festival, the Castle will undo its history of executions
        and torture.
Our autumn homepage will feature a release of historic /
        celebrity prisoners:

- The Lord of the Isles
- Jacobites, Covenanters, Stuarts, Catholics,
- Parliamentarians
- Red Clydesiders
- The 4,000 witches burnt to death on the Esplanade

The slightest breeze will lift and carry each one over the
    battlements,
letting them drift down, settling them upon this official
stretch of reflected sky.

There, weightless as human hope itself,
they'll walk upon water –
taking their first few steps on the road to freedom.

Sometimes Edinburgh's considered rather unwelcoming. How very
wrong this is. Even in the sound and cadence of the city's place-
names we can sense the playfulness and affectionate warmth of our
nation's capital.

Edinburgh Love Song

Ye're richt Dalmahoy whenever ye see her,
fair Bingham fer aa the Pleasance ye'll gie her.
She's Roseburn, she's Shandon – but where can ye take her
fer some Ravelstone, Gracemount an then Goldenacre?

There's a few in this city wi mair censure than pity,
some Pilrig or Drylaw will aye get nit-picky
– they'll Ratho ye baith in the name o her honour,
they'll Riccarton, Broughton and Brunstane upon her,
they'll Stockbridge and Tron her
if ye dinna act true.

But pey them nae heed – fer shairly she'll Meadowbank
always wi you!